Who Killed Marta Ugarte?

Memorial and grave site, Atacama Desert

Who Killed Marta Ugarte?

Poems in memory of the victims
of Augusto Pinochet

Jeanne-Marie Osterman

Jeanne-Marie Osterman
September 2023

Broadstone

Copyright © 2023 by Jeanne-Marie Osterman

Library of Congress Control No. 2023940911

ISBN 978-1-956782-47-9

Photographs not otherwise credited
are by the author

Design by Larry W. Moore

Front cover design by Maria Rodriguez Mazon

Used by permission of Museum of Memory and Human Rights, Chile:

Front cover photo/photo on page 4
Marta Ugarte
Román Ugarte Family Collection

Photo, page 8
"María de la Memoria," 2009
Claudio Di Girolamo Collection

Photo, page 38
"La cueca sola"
Isabel Morel Collection

Broadstone Books
An Imprint of
Broadstone Media LLC
418 Ann Street
Frankfort, KY 40601-1929
BroadstoneBooks.com

On September 11, 1973, the democratically-elected government of Chile was overthrown by a military coup d'etat.

The resulting dictatorship of General Augusto Pinochet was one of the most brutal in modern history. During his 17-year regime, tens of thousands of Chileans were tortured, more than 200,000 forced into exile, and over 3,000 murdered or "disappeared." In Pinochet's *Caravana de la Muerte* (Caravan of Death), scores of public officials were tortured, executed, and thrown into common graves. Hundreds of others were weighted with pieces of railroad track, bagged in canvas, and dropped from helicopters into the Pacific Ocean.

Fifty years later, we have good reason to remember Chile—both for those who suffered, and for the democracy they lost.

Contents

Prologue / ix

Hard Work / 3
Open Letter to Marta Ugarte / 5
Romo / 7
A Story Told in Pieces / 9
Testimony / 10
Marta / 11
Villa Grimaldi / 13
When / 14

How to Shoot Your Own Death / 17
The Testimony of Burgos Espejo / 18
Volodya / 19
Venda Sexy / 21
In the Kitchen with DINA / 22
Because an Agent Has His Side of the Story, Too / 23

Which Santiago de Chile Did I Love Most? / 27

Who Am I / 31
Por Siempre / 33
Ossuary / 36
Mothers of the Atacama / 37
What I Remember about el Museo de la Memoria / 41
One Pearl Button / 42
Calle Londres #38 / 45
Found at Villa Grimaldi / 47

Notes / 52
Acknowledgments / 53

Prologue

How long and lonely the rocky shore

How blue the sea,

    an open eye,

where helicopters hovered and dropped the bodies

How each was tied to a length of rail

How one corpse came loose and drifted to shore

How years later divers discovered the rusted rails,
    one with a shirt button still attached

∼

Hundreds more found in the Atacama Desert

There are photographs—

Here, a closeup of the pockmarked earth—
    it looks like another planet

Here, a plastic spoon used to search for shards

Here, a man digs with his hands

Here, two diggers lie next to each other showing the camera
    how two bodies were buried together

∼

In a laboratory in the city,
*　　　an anthropologist sifts through bags of sand*

With a paintbrush she dusts off bits of bone,
*　　　parts of a puzzle—*

a face reimagined through the shape of a skull

It's difficult to find missing prisoners, given that the aim was exactly that: to make them disappear without leaving a trace.

—Elizabeth Lira,
　　Alberto Hurtado University, Santiago, Chile

Pieces of railroad track found by divers off the coast of Chile. Many of Pinochet's victims were "disappeared" by tying them to heavy lengths of track and dropping them from helicopters into the Pacific Ocean.

Hard Work

The mechanics are at the prison
waiting for the Puma to land.

Minutes to make safety checks,
refuel, load freight. Hard work

hauling slack bodies, one dead
per bag, each tied to iron track.

Most long as a man, some shorter,
the body broken. One bag still

moving—a job unfinished.

Marta Ugarte

Open Letter to Marta Ugarte

> *Marta Lidia Ugarte Román, a teacher, was one of the many political prisoners kidnapped, murdered, and dropped into the Pacific Ocean by the Pinochet regime.*

I wasn't a believer in afterlives,
        miracles, till I read
about you, *desaparecida*,

appearing to a fisherman
        at La Ballena Beach.
Apologies—I'm late in saying this,

I know: songs, poems, plays written,
        quilts, murals made
in your memory, and you'd probably

just like to rest in peace.
        But I can't help myself—
want you to know we remember

that September day, when Pincetti
        injected you with pentothal
and took you for dead—

were you awake when they tied you
        to 30 kilos of iron track
and bagged you in a potato sack?

Like one of a dozen cocoons
        stacked at the prison gate,
did you feel the other bodies

grow cold? And when the guards
        saw you were still alive,
did they curse you for your strength?

Or themselves, for being unable
        to kill a woman so small?
We remember too, how

they used the wire
        that tied you to the track
to strangle you, and how

untied from the track, you didn't sink
        when they dropped you
into the Pacific.

I think of you as *una mariposa*,
        still in your chrysalis—
metamorphosis when they pushed you

from the helicopter into the sky.
        How did it feel, Marta, to fly,
after days in a cell so small

you had to stand while waiting
        for the next round of torture?
I see you land on ocean surface,

and as butterflies are carried
        on a breath of wind,
you were carried by a current to shore.

When the fisherman found you,
        your eyes were open.

Romo

Would you do it again? Would you do it the same way?

Sure, I'd do the same and more. I was always arguing,

Don't leave that person alive!

There will be consequences.

As for throwing the prisoners into the sea…

The crater of a volcano would be better.

Who'd go looking for them there?

What will your epitaph say? "Here lies the hangman, the torturer, the murderer?"

Logical, logical. I accept that.

But for me it was a positive thing.

Retrato de familia

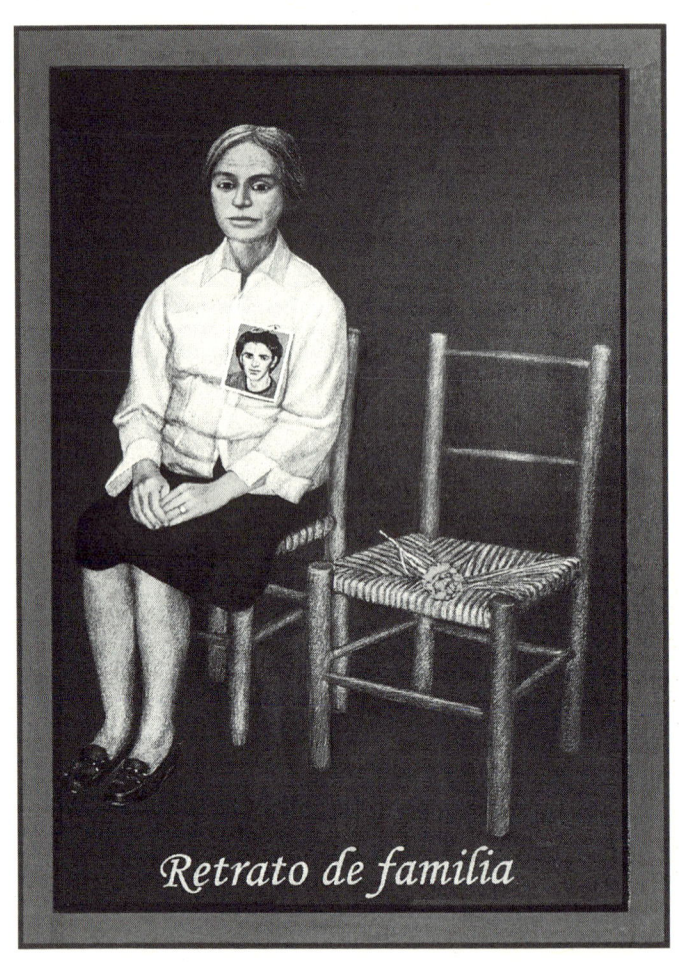

"Family Portrait"

A Story Told in Pieces

of track

    tied to prisoners

    to make them sink

    in the Pacific

of bodies

    found in the Atacama

    foot still in its shoe

    finger bone wearing a ring

of bones

    in bags

    human jigsaw

    to be solved by anthropologists

of families

    [disappeared]

of testimony

    too hard to hold in

Testimony

The helicopter was coming,
        the retired guard tells the judge.

The General commanded us—
        Get the bodies into bags!

We couldn't keep the helicopter waiting—
        the schedule, the fuel spent, the noise—

so we used the wire that tied Marta to the track
        to strangle her.

Marta

Ever the teacher,
your body is a curriculum
for atrocity—
twenty extracted nails
seven broken ribs
one ruptured spleen
two dislocated hips
thirty-six lash marks, burn marks
sinnúmero
ocho días in Villa Grimaldi

"Here's how they torture in Chile"
From Chile's National Commission Against Torture

Villa Grimaldi
After Gonzalo Millán

The tower is divided into cells
The cells are beneath the chamber
The chamber holds *la parrilla*
La parrilla is Spanish for grill
The prisoner is tied to the grill
The grill is tied to the current
The switch is turned
The current hums

The doctor inserts the needle
The mechanics cut the wire into lengths
The doves look on from the tower
The bodies are wired to the tracks
The tracks are put into potato sacks
The potato sacks are stacked by the gate
The Puma lands
The doves fly

When
After Pablo Neruda's "Cuándo de Chile"

cargo / *cuerpos*
plan / Pinochet

prisoners / pieces
bodies in burlap bags

pilots / pick up
Puma / *el Pacifico*

Oh, Chile,
long petal
of loss
and loneliness

when
oh when and when
oh when
will they come home again?

How to Shoot Your Own Death
> *I am a camera with its shutter open, quite passive, recording, not thinking.*
> —Christopher Isherwood, *Berlin Stories*

Soldiers, street corner, Santiago de Chile, June 29, 1973

Heads in helmets, hands holding automatic weapons, armored vehicle in frame

¡Para! ¡Aléjate! Stop! Get away!

                [BLAM!]

Man holding me loses grip, tumbles to cobblestones

I catch a patch of jeans, plaid shirt, a shoelace

Land on pavement pointed at soldier who fired

Expression

Nothing

The Testimony of Burgos Espejo

I was eleven when I saw my brother shot at our front door

I was eleven when I saw my brother shot at

I was eleven when I saw my brother

I was eleven when I saw

I was eleven

I was

was

Volodya

cry of women
howl of dog
his name
Volodya
German Shepherd
caged in
basement
how did they train him
to rape
female prisoners
rewarded each time
with raw meat
that's how
they broke her
she was raped
by a dog

                    by a dog
                    she was raped
                    they broke her
                    that's how
                    with raw meat
                    rewarded each time
                    female prisoners
                    to rape
                    how did they train him
                    basement
                    caged in
                    German Shepherd
                    Volodya
                    his name
                    howl of dog
                    cry of women

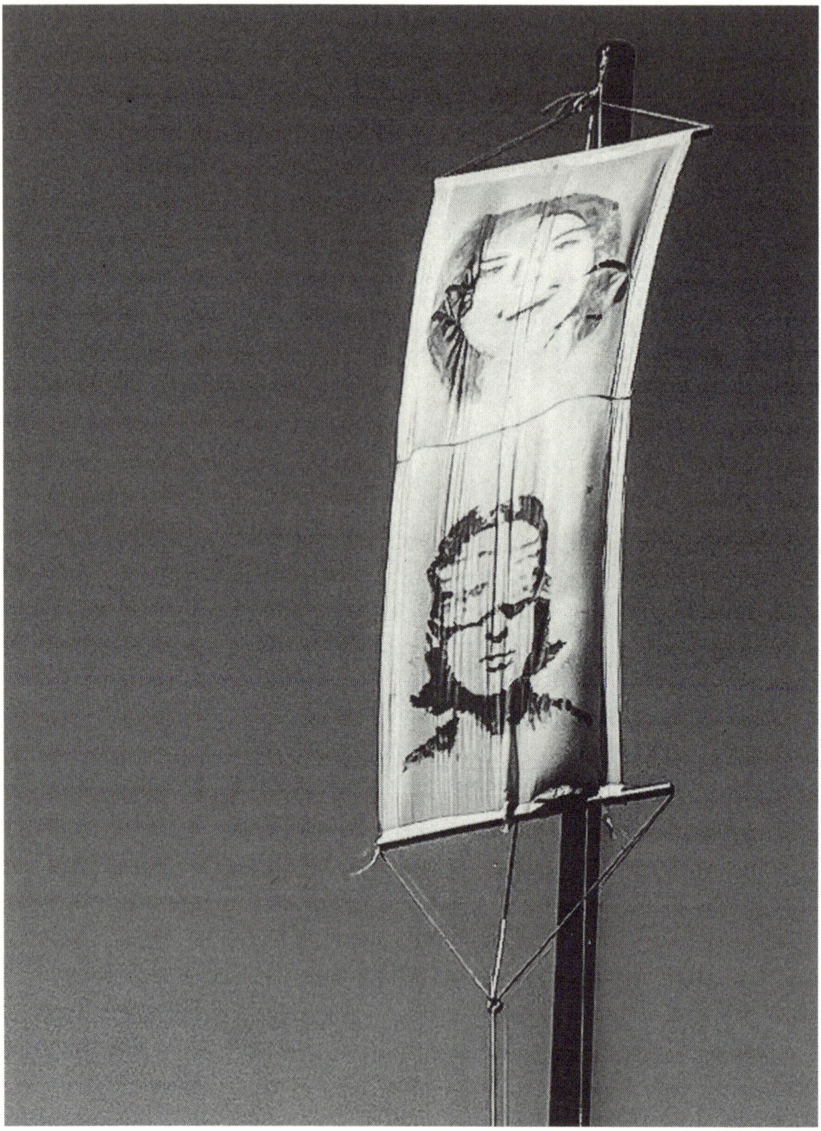

Venda Sexy

just a house
an ordinary house
garden of bellflowers
jasmine, herb of the worm
high fence
bright orange paint
balcony, sliding glass doors

Venda Sexy,
sexy blindfold,
name given by guards
for how it happened here—
eyes bandaged
while raped by agent
or dog

Not all sexy—
beatings, hangings,
electrical shocks
deafening music
to drown out screams

earning it a second name—
La Discoteca

A group of survivors
wanted to make it a memorial.
Others wanted to tear it down.
The compromise?
A tile
in the sidewalk.
Residents complained.

In the Kitchen with DINA[1]
After pastel de choclo, traditional recipe of Chile

Preheat: Propaganda, shortages
oil, flour, salt. Grease well, CIA
funds: pay liberally workers to strike.
Method: Tear husks from ears hang
from ceiling well-sharpened knife.
Repeat white flesh of onion, burn.
Blister. Meat grind till fine red till
blood. Pummel. Olives black eyes
pitted flatten butt-end of knife. *Ají*,
hot pepper, generous mix well lips
genitals anus. Sweeten, raisins as
needed, breaks down resistance.
Whip. Let stand five days dark air-
less space. Make a fist. Punch down
dough, OK to let rise, punch till no
more rise. Snap to grill high heat.
Roll flat wrap tight clean area well.

[1]Dirección de Inteligencia Nacional (National Intelligence Directorate), Pinochet's secret police

Because an Agent Has His Side of the Story, Too

It was cold there at Chacabuco, very cold
I was just one of hundreds
I was forced into it
I only got a small serving of soup
I was just a squaddie
I was made to sing the anthem, morning till night
The hours were long—eight to six-thirty
Either too hot or too cold
If the general didn't like something, I was punished
If I didn't torture a prisoner enough, I had to do it over
If we didn't kill them, we would be killed
I had to force heads into buckets of urine
I had to clean a cell where five prisoners were held
I had to deliver the blindfolds
I had to listen to the women being raped
I had to listen to the cueca played all night long, louder than their screams
It was my job
I had to deliver #345 to Colonia Dignidad where he was killed while I ate dinner
I didn't even have shoes
I had to put them on a list to be killed
I had to put them on a list to declare them dead
I had to clean the tower which was the place to be killed

I was told I was saving my country

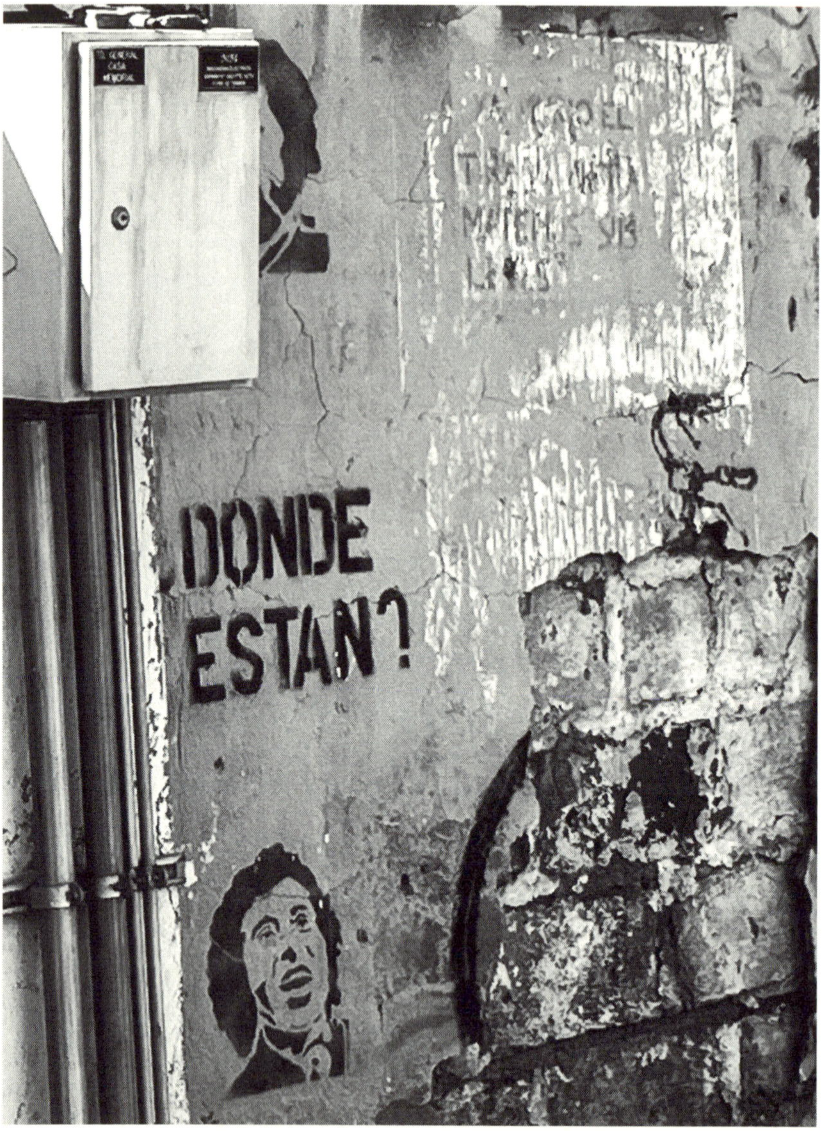
DONDE
ESTAN?

Which Santiago de Chile Did I Love Most?

City of man playing Miles in Bustamonte Park, gingerly and off-key

City of backstreet cafes where bootlegged tapes outlawed by dictatorship were played anyway, 1974–1990

City of La Chascona, Neruda's house, now a museum, where thousands gathered days after he died, to pay their respects, violating curfew, risking death

City of Rio Mapocho, graffiti along embankments still asking, *¿Dónde están?*

City of Estadio Victor Jara, stadium named for folk singer machine-gunned to death for writing *somos cinco mil*—we are five thousand—the number of political prisoners he was held with there

City of La Moneda Presidential Palace, where Salvador Allende, minutes before ending his own life, said, *Go forward knowing that, sooner rather than later, the great avenues will open again where free men will walk to build a better society*

City of kudzu-covered house in Lastarria—blacked-out windows like eyes, door a screaming mouth

City of Condorito, cartoon bird symbol of Chile, who in final frame always falls down ¡PLOP! in yet another self-inflicted misfortune

City of Violeta Parra, whose paintings and tapestries sing as brightly as her song, *Gracias a la Vida*

City of Gabriela Mistral, poet of corn, wine, water, and sand, whose songs of tenderness are sung by Chilean children

City of Iglesia de San Francisco, oldest Catholic church in Chile, its cloister littered with broken mannequins

City of democratically-elected president's bomb-shattered glasses, left lens missing, displayed in a vitrine

City of stray dogs—hundreds and hundreds of them—walking shoulder to shoulder, sniffing the cobblestones and all who pass, on guard for something only dogs can sense

City, both blood-soaked and beautiful, city that on rare days when smog lifts and the Andes do that thing that happens when sunlight hits snow, fusillade of white light that shouts ¡mírame, mírame! making you look up and think of all she's survived, and you love her, love her

… I think how little we can hold in mind, how everything is constantly lapsing into oblivion with every extinguished life, how the world is, as it were, draining itself, in that the history of countless places and objects which themselves have no power of memory is never heard, never described or passed on.

—W. G. Sebald

Who Am I

to be a voice for the disappeared,
fifty years later,
put into words wounds
of a country not my own,
language not my own, wounds

from guns of country, my own—
serial numbers scrubbed out with acid,
junta by telex
from Henry Kissinger
to CIA Station House in Santiago?

Poetry of witness—I witness
only to television reports
sent by satellite morning of September 11, 1973,
bombs dropping on presidential palace,
haze of static, lens shaking
to black

Survivor of torture and imprisonment at Chile's National Stadium. He was imprisoned here as a university student in 1973.

Por Siempre

Under the sidewalks,
thousands of sleeping souls—
tortured and killed in secret,
the only eye witnesses, the perpetrators—

> *We liked to kill them slowly, cut off*
> *an arm, a leg, then the sexual organs,*
> *finishing them off with a gun…*

~

Recordar, to remember

    re, to return

        cordar, from *corazón*, the heart

            to return to the heart

~

Is memory words?
Or a ghost who walks the streets?

~

The houses along Calle Londres—so close they appear to be holding hands. Names of the victims, mostly women, engraved in the sidewalk outside #38, center for detention and torture, now an attraction at dark-tourist.com—

Some rooms out of bounds to visitors. A work in progress. The designated memorial space has been whitewashed which contributes to the eerie atmosphere.

∼

Disappeared—
the electrical fences and watchtowers of Chacabuco
the bloodstains on the walls of Villa Grimaldi
the metal coils of *la parrilla*
the volt batteries and blindfolds of *Venda Sexy*
the serial numbers on weapons sent by Henry Kissinger
the 1,170 detention camps
the 17 torture centers
the 3,197 *muertos*

Still here—
the black ink of redaction on over 250,000 pages of U.S. government files

∼

What is remembrance?
Roses left by school children on the cobblestones of La Moneda?
Mothers still searching the Atacama for bones?
A band marches down O'Higgins Boulevard
playing the anthem of *Partido Unidad*.
A man in a wheelchair flashes the peace sign.
Two older women link arms and smile.
Most don't react. Seventeen years of trying
to forget has frozen their faces forever.

∽

A ceramic plaque at the gate of Villa Grimaldi reads,
Esta puerta permanecerá cerrada por siempre.

Ossuary

age

age sex

age sex stature

age sex stature make a picture

age sex stature make a picture of someone who once was

Mothers of the Atacama

I.

A woman finds
her brother's foot,
still in its shoe,
a few teeth,
piece of forehead—
takes shoe home
in a bag, sits with it
through the night.

II.

If they put them in the desert, we'll find them.
If they put them in an abandoned mine, we'll find them.
If they threw them into Rio Mapocho, we'll find them.
If they dropped them into a ditch, we'll find them.
If they threw them into a fiery volcano, we'll find them.
If they crushed them, ground them, burned them to ash, we'll find them.
If they tied them to iron rails and dropped them into the sea,
    we will bring them to the surface.

III.

We are the lowest of the low.
We are dogs—
Chile's leprosy.
The problem that won't go away,
    won't let them forget.

IV.

Atacama,
genius of preservation,
depository of bones
crushed by blows,
blown up with dynamite,
layers of skeletons lie within,
waiting to tell their story.

V.

Silently they go about it,
in small groups, searching,
shovels so short
they're on their knees.

They avoid the *lomas*,
low hills where fog feeds
a flower, an insect,
creates life—
concentrating on places
where there is no life
to break down a body,
consume the bones.

They grid off the desert
with stones and string,
hoping to find
one shard, hoping
to no longer need hope.

VI.

She finds a tiny shard,
holds it in her palm,
with a fingertip
turns it over
and over.

VII.

In parts of the Atacama where there is no rainfall,
farmers suspend nets in the air to catch clouds
rolling in from the Pacific. Tiny droplets of moisture
collect on the fibers and trickle down the skeins into
pipes that lead to small reservoirs. From nothing,
something. From shards, *los desaparecidos* reappear.

Children paying tribute to the disappeared at Museum of Memory and Human Rights, Chile

What I Remember about el Museo de la Memoria

I remember the map, long as a freight train, Chile laid on its side, callouts
    pinpointing concentration camps, Calama to Punta Arenas

I remember the three-story wall of 1,801 photographs of the disappeared and
    dead, and my ridiculous notion that they could see me

I remember the children kneeling and lighting candles, and my thinking that
    even though they couldn't possibly remember what had happened
    here, there was still this reverence, and how that made me feel hope

I remember the diaries of Pinochet's victims, their poetry of how to survive,
    drawings of cages they were kept in, crouched like cats

I remember the tools of the torturers, and feeling grateful that someone had
    saved these artifacts of a humanity gone mad, and I remember loving
    that so many were willing to look at what they can't possibly love or
    want to remember

And I remember thinking that in a country accused of forgetting, it was all
    here to remember, and how these memories allow us to live in the
    present because without memories we don't live anywhere

One Pearl Button

embedded in track
mother of pearl
born of abalone
returned to the sea
by soldiers of Pinochet

One pearl button
lodged in a dent
of iron track
tied to a man's
thoracic cage

One pearl button
engraved a message
in iron rail
found by divers
and brought to a judge

One pearl button
multicolored nacre
reflecting light
on the depth
of their crimes

One pearl button
teardrop
in an ocean
of death

One pearl button
expanding
like a wave

One pearl button
once held together
someone's shirt
the someone
dissolved in the sea

#NOMASIMPUNIDAD

Londres 38
espacio de memorias

GIANA ROSETTA PALLINI GONZÁLEZ

21 años, militante del MIR

Nació en Talca, casada, un hijo, estudiante de Pedagogía en Historia y Geografía. Fue detenida el 15 de agosto de 1974, expulsada del país en marzo de 1975, murió el 2 de agosto de ese año a consecuencia de las torturas sufridas.

Giana Rosetta Pallini González, 21, university student and mother who was kidnapped and held at Londres 38. After months of interrogation and torture, she was sent out of the country where she died of her injuries.

Calle Londres #38

Located in an upscale neighborhood, this converted brick house was a holding station for female inmates en route to concentration camps. None of the high-tech appeal of Santiago's Museo de la Memoria y los Derechos Humanos, but an authentic detention center nonetheless.

An attendant will direct you to a stairway—the same one new inmates were taken up blindfolded. Rooms upstairs have been emptied and whitewashed, but there are some vaguely suggestive remnants—pipes protruding from walls, clipped wires covered with plaster, ghost of an iron bed.

On view are photographs of some of the women who were tortured here. Captions indicate name, age, date disappeared or murdered. All but one were students. As you leave, check out the lively neighborhood cafe next door. Don't miss the pastries. They're exceptional.

"Torture and interrogation room"
Wall text at Londres 38, Santiago

"Torture room, electrified metal beds, the grill"
Mosaic at Parque por la Paz,
the former Villa Grimaldi detention center, Santiago

Found At Villa Grimaldi
After David Allen Sullivan

Iron track,
        3-foot lengths,
        rusted;

Potato sacks,
        SUPERAVIT—
        surplus;

Twenty spools of wire,
        cutters;

Calipers,
        paean to dried blood,
        gaping;

Fingernails,
        extracted,
        numerous;

Chalkboard,
        list / schedule /
        extermination;

Notebook,
        dog-eared,
        death count;

Truck,
        tire treads,
        flesh-embedded;

Electrical wire,
        battery, stopwatch;

MIR pamphlet,
    EVIDENCIA;

Condorito,
    comic book—
    ¡PLOP!

Restraint chair,
    USA;

Buckets,
    feces-
    urine-stained;

Syringe, needle,
    ghost of a fist;

Toy shooting gallery,
    battered duck;

Handbook, torture—
    logo: *Luftwaffe*;

Swimsuit,
    child size;

Coffee cup, decal:
    Caravana de la Muerte;

Scent of oranges,
    electrical charge;

Cages,
    rat skeletons,
    (torture);

Empty space,
> shadow of guard's eye;

Diary,
> DINA—
> disappearing ink;

T-shirt,
> *Team Pinochet*;

Echo,
> cry of comrade
> forced to watch;

Mourning doves,
> silent;

Aftershave, shoe polish,
> invitation to military ball;

Hood,
> bloodstained;

Handkerchief,
> tearstained;

Passersby,
> blinders,
> earplugs

*Photos of the disappeared,
Museum of Memory and Human Rights, Chile*

... the calm metal instrument of my voice will no longer reach you. It does not matter. You will continue hearing it.

—Salvador Allende, September 11, 1973

Notes

Elizabeth Lira quotation from *theguardian.com*, August 14, 2019, "'Where Are they?': families search for Chile's disappeared prisoners," sourced August 4, 2022.

"Romo." Adapted from an interview with Osvaldo Romo, DINA Agent, 1973-1990. https://en.wikipedia.org/wiki/Osvaldo_Romo, sourced January 4, 2022.

"The Testimony of Burgos Espejo." Inspired by an article in *Aljazeera*, December 17, 2021, "'Still a lot of pain': Dictatorship victims haunt Chile election," by Sandra Cuffe.

"Because an Agent Has His Side of the Story, Too." Based on testimony of Pinochet ex-agent as reported in "Music and Torture in Chilean Detention Centers: Conversations with an Ex-Agent of Pinochet's Secret Police," by Katia Chornik, *World of Music*, 2013.

W. G. Sebald quotation from *Austerlitz*, Modern Library, 2011.

"*Por Siempre*." Quotation adapted from testimony of Gen. Joaquin Lagos, reported in *theguardian.com*, January 27, 2001, "Pinochet tied to massacre," sourced January 30, 2023.

"Mothers of the Atacama." Details on extracting water droplets from fog draws on description of same in the novel, *Apeirogon*, by Colum McCann, Random House, 2020.

Acknowledgments

I am greatly indebted to the films of Patricio Guzmán. His documentaries, *The Battle of Chile* (1975, 1976 & 1978), *Obstinate Memory* (1997), and *Nostalgia for the Light* (2010), included footage of events referred to in these poems, as well as interviews with those who lived through them. More than a source of information, Guzmán's films were an inspiration.

Deepest admiration for the investigative reporting of Peter Kornbluh. His book, *The Pinochet File: A Declassified Dossier on Atrocity and Accountability* (The New Press, 2013 updated edition), was an invaluable resource. This comprehensive and meticulously detailed report documents both the workings of the Pinochet dictatorship and the U.S. role in putting him into power.

Gratitude to staff members at Museo de la Memoria y los Derechos Humanos, who were happy to answer my questions.

Thanks to poets Matthew Lippman and TJ Beitelman, whose comments and encouragement helped me complete this manuscript.

Thanks to The Writers Colony at Dairy Hollow for the time and space.

Huge thanks to Larry Moore of Broadstone Books for believing in this manuscript and bringing it to life.

Thank you, Felipe, Fernando, Leonides, and Tito for your songs, stories, and friendship.

About the Author

Jeanne-Marie Osterman is the author of three collections of poetry: *Shellback* (Paloma Press), named by *Kirkus Reviews* one of the top 100 indie press books of 2021; *All Animals Want the Same Things*, winner of the Slipstream 34th Annual Poetry Chapbook Competition; and *There's a Hum* (Finishing Line Press, 2018). Her poems have appeared in *Borderlands*, *45th Parallel*, *The Madison Review*, *New Ohio Review*, and other journals, and in 2018 she was a finalist for the Joy Harjo Poetry Prize. A native of the Pacific Northwest, Jeanne-Marie resides in New York City where she is poetry editor for *Cagibi*, an online journal of poetry and prose. Visit her online at ostermanpoetry.com